The Greatest Bible Stories Ever Told
Friendship & Kindness

Stephen Elkins
AUTHOR

Tim O'Connor
ILLUSTRATIONS

BROADMAN
& HOLMAN
PUBLISHERS
NASHVILLE, TENNESSEE

RUTH AND NAOMI

Ruth 1:16 Where you go I will go, where you stay I will stay. Your people will be my people and your God my God.

The judges were ruling Israel in the days when a terrible famine came. A man named Elimelech, his wife Naomi, and their two sons left Bethlehem and moved to Moab where there was plenty of food. While in Moab, Elimelech died, leaving Naomi alone with two sons. Sometime later, her sons married Moabite women named Orpah and Ruth.

They lived as a happy family for about ten years, and then both of her sons died. When Naomi learned that the famine in Judah had ended, she prepared to leave Moab and return home. Ruth and Orpah walked with Naomi part of the way because they loved her very much. Naomi said, "Each of you must go back to your mother's house. May the Lord show kindness to you."

Orpah returned home to her mother, but Ruth said, "Where you go I will go. Your people will be my people, and your God my God."

So the two women traveled on to Bethlehem where the barley harvest had just begun. It was a custom in those days that the poor would follow behind the harvesters and pick up any barley left behind.
It was called "gleaning."

"I will go to the fields and glean," Ruth told Naomi. Ruth began working in a field owned by a man named Boaz, a relative of Naomi's.

Boaz noticed how hard Ruth was working and asked who she was. "She's a young woman from Moab who returned with Naomi," answered the foreman. Boaz liked Ruth and said, "Please stay close by and do not glean anywhere else. Stay near the other women and I'll make sure you are protected."

Ruth bowed and said, "Why are you being so kind to me?" Boaz replied, "I've heard how you left your home to care for Naomi. May the Lord bless you for what you have done."

Boaz helped Ruth in many ways. He made sure that she had enough to eat. He admired her very much because she always took care of Naomi. Boaz fell in love with Ruth and asked her to marry him. They were married one sunny day and soon a baby named Obed was born. He would be the father of Jesse who would be the father of David, the king of Israel. Naomi continued to live with Ruth and Boaz, and was very happy.

Affirmation: I will be a friend to others!

BRAVE AND BEAUTIFUL QUEEN

Esther 4:14 And who knows but that you have come to royal position for such a time as this?

Once, in the city of Susa, the capital of Persia, great King Xerxes gave a banquet in honor of his many governors. As the banquet went on, King Xerxes called for Vashti the queen. "Place the royal crown on Vashti's head and bring her to me," commanded the king, for she was very beautiful.

When Queen Vashti refused to come, the king was very angry. He sent Vashti away and ordered a nationwide search for a new queen.

Now there was a Jewish man named Mordecai who also lived in Persia. He had a beautiful cousin named Esther. In obedience to the king's order, Esther was taken to the king's palace. Mordecai asked her to tell no one that she was Jewish.

When the king saw Esther, he loved her. He set the royal crown on her head and made her the new queen.

One day Mordecai was sitting at the king's gate waiting to see Esther. He heard two soldiers planning to kill the king. Mordecai told Esther, who in turn, told the king.

"Mordecai has told me of a plot to kill you, my King!" said Esther. The king had the two men arrested and they were found guilty. Mordecai had saved the king's life and it was written down in the history books.

After this, King Xerxes honored Haman by making him second in command of Persia. Haman was a very proud man and at the king's order everyone was to bow before him. But Mordecai would bow to no one except the Lord. This angered Haman. When he later found out that Mordecai was an Israelite, he began to look for a way to destroy them all. Then he came up with an evil plan.

Haman went to King Xerxes and said, "There are people in your kingdom who do not obey your laws, O King, but rather God's laws. This is not good for us. Therefore, let us send soldiers to kill them." The king agreed, so Haman sent out an order to kill the Jews.

When Mordecai heard about Haman's evil plan, he sent word to Esther. "Perhaps God has made you Queen of Persia for such a time as this. Maybe He will use you to save His people."

Then Esther sent word back to Mordecai. "Gather all the Jews in Susa and pray for three days. Though it's against the law for me to go to the king, I will do so. Pray that the king will have mercy and stop Haman's evil plan." Mordecai did as Esther asked.

On the third day, Esther prepared
a banquet and only invited the king and Haman.
"What can I do for you?" the king asked. "Name it
and it will be done." Esther spoke, "Will you and
Haman come tomorrow to another special banquet?
Then I will tell you both."

As Haman left, he again passed Mordecai at the gate.
Again, Mordecai refused to bow. Haman, in his anger,
decided to start building the place where Mordecai would be
executed. That night, as the king was reading the history
book, he discovered he had not honored Mordecai for saving
his life. He called Haman and said, "I want to honor a special
man. What should I do?"

Haman thought he was the man to be honored, so he said, "Let him wear the royal robe and be put on the king's horse and lead him through the city proclaiming, 'The king is honoring this man!'" So Haman was asked to honor Mordecai in this way. Haman was furious.

Later, Haman and the king went to dine with Esther. "What is your request? Tell me and it shall be yours," said the king to Esther. "O King, spare me and the life of my people."

"Spare you? You are the queen!" said the king. "Yes," said Esther, "but I am also a Jew. And there is a man in the kingdom who wants to kill all of the Jews."

"Who is this man?" asked the king. "Haman," she replied. "He is an evil man."

The king was furious and that night Haman was hanged on the very gallows he had built for Mordecai. God's people were saved!

Affirmation: I will kneel and pray to God alone!

KINDHEARTED KING

2 Samuel 22:4 I (will) call upon the Lord, who is worthy to be praised.

During a fierce battle with the Philistine army, King Saul found his army outnumbered and fled. Saul and his three sons, including Jonathan, were all killed that day. David became the new king of Israel.

David did not know that Jonathan, his dearest friend, had a five-year-old son named Mephibosheth. In that day when a new king came to the throne, he would search for the children of the old king and have them sent away or killed so they could never be king. That is why Mephibosheth's nurse took the boy and fled for safety. In her haste, she stumbled and dropped the little boy, crippling him for life.

One day, King David asked if any of Saul's family was alive. He wanted to show them kindness because of his promise to Jonathan. A former servant to Saul named Ziba told him Jonathan's crippled son Mephibosheth was indeed alive. David sent for him and he was brought to the palace. Mephibosheth must have thought David was going to kill him. He fell on his face and cried, "Here is your servant."

But David said, "Don't be afraid. I will give back to you all the land your grandfather Saul owned and you shall always be welcome at my dinner table." Because of David's kindness, Mephibosheth became a part of the king's family.

Affirmation: I will show kindness to others!

POOR LITTLE RICH BOY

Micah 4:2 Let us go up to the mountain of the Lord ... He will teach us his ways.

Micah was a great prophet of the Lord who stood up for the poor in Israel. Micah preached against rich rulers who were stealing land from the poor and not listening to their cries for help. Micah taught the people, "Each of us must do what is right before God. We must show kindness and forgive one another. Turn to the Lord and tell Him all the things you have done wrong, then God will forgive you. The Lord will be your light."

Affirmation: I will tell others about God's love!

ROOFTOP MIRACLE

Mark 2:5   When Jesus saw their faith, he said to the paralytic, "Son, your sins are forgiven."

One day, Jesus was teaching in a home in Capernaum. The crowd grew so big that there was no room to stand inside. Even the doorways were jammed with people.

Some men came to see Jesus that day. They brought their friend who was sick and could not move. They believed that Jesus would heal him. "This crowd is too big," they said. "How will our friend ever see Jesus?" Then they had an idea!

The four men carried their friend, who lay on a mat, up to the roof. They began tearing away the rooftop to make a large hole right above Jesus! Then they lowered their friend down through the hole and he came to rest right in front of the Lord. Jesus knew these men must have great faith to do such a thing. So He said to the sick man, "Your sins are forgiven. Get up, take your mat, and go home."

Suddenly the man felt strength coming back into his arms and legs. He raised up ... he could move! Then he leaped off the mat and walked right through the crowd praising God!

Jesus had taken away his sickness and his sin, all in one miracle moment! This amazed everyone and they praised God, giving thanks saying, "We have never seen anything like this."

Affirmation: I will lead my friends to Jesus!

THE CALL OF THE DISCIPLES

Mark 1:17 Come, follow me and I will make you fishers of men.

Mark was a friend of Peter's who wrote down some of the stories Peter told about Jesus. One day as Jesus was walking beside the Sea of Galilee, He saw Peter and Peter's brother, Andrew. They were fishermen. "Come follow Me," Jesus said, "and I will make you fishers of men." At once they left their fishing nets and followed Him.

When they had gone a little further, they met James and his brother John who were also fishermen. As they were fixing their nets, Jesus said, "Come follow Me."

Without delay, they left their boat and followed Jesus.

Sometime later, Jesus had called twelve men to be His disciples. They would spend time with Him and learn God's Word. Then someday they would go out and preach the good news! They were Peter, Andrew, James, John, Philip, Bartholomew, Matthew, Thomas, another James, Thaddaeus, Simon, and Judas.

Affirmation: I want to be a disciple of Jesus too!

THE GOOD SAMARITAN

Luke 10:36   "Which of these three do you think was a neighbor to the man who fell into the hands of robbers?"

Once a lawyer asked Jesus this tricky question, "If we are to love our neighbor as ourselves, who then is our neighbor?" Jesus answered, "A man was traveling from Jerusalem to Jericho when he was attacked by robbers. They took everything he had. They beat him up and left him by the roadside nearly dead. Soon, a priest came along. But when he saw the man, he passed by on the other side of the road.

Another church worker came along. But seeing the man, he
too, passed him by without helping him. But then came a
Samaritan. He was from another country. But when he
saw the man hurt and bleeding, he stopped and helped him.
He bandaged his wounds, put him on his own donkey and
took him to an inn. There he cared for the man.

The next day, he took two silver coins and gave them to the innkeeper. The Samaritan said, 'Take care of this man and if you spend more than this, I will repay you.'"

Then Jesus said to the lawyer, "Which one of the three men was a good neighbor?" The lawyer answered, "Why, the one who helped him!" "Go and do likewise," Jesus told him.

Affirmation: I will be a good neighbor!

WALKING WITH GOD

1 John 4:7 Love one another, for love comes from God.

John tells us that if we are to walk with God, we must walk in the light. For God is light. We are to be honest when we speak and loving to those in need. If we walk in the light, Satan, that prince of darkness, can never harm us. John also reminds us that God is love. "Dear children, let us not love with words, but with action and truth." If we walk in the light and in His love, surely we will walk with Jesus forever in heaven.

That's a mighty promise!

Affirmation: I will walk with Jesus!

GOD'S KIND OF LOVE

1 Corinthians 13:4 Love is patient, love is kind.

There was a brand new group of Christians who started a church in the great city of Corinth, Greece. Corinth was full of idol worshipers and Paul had journeyed there many times to preach the good news of Jesus Christ. In one of his letters written to this growing church, he explained the meaning of "God's kind of Love." He wrote: "If I could speak with the words of an angel, but had no love inside my heart, I would only be making noise like a clanging cymbal.

If I knew all there was to know and could move mountains with my faith, I would still have an empty heart without love. If I gave everything I own to the poor, I would gain nothing if it wasn't given in love. When we have God's kind of love in our hearts, we are willing to be patient with others. When we have God's kind of love in our hearts, we don't become jealous of others, wanting what they may have.

When we have God's kind of love in our hearts, we never hurt anyone's feelings by being rude, and we always forgive others. When we have God's love in our hearts, we think of others first, not ourselves. We stay away from bad things and seek to do good things. When we have God's kind of love inside, we protect the helpless, and hope for the good. God's kind of love keeps on loving no matter what happens. That's why God's love is the greatest gift we can give to others."

Affirmation: I will show God's kind of love!

ONESIMUS

Philemon 1:4 (I always thank God as) I remember you in my prayers.

Paul was arrested for preaching the gospel while in the city of Rome. This letter was written from his prison cell to a wealthy friend named Philemon. Philemon had a slave named Onesimus who had stolen from him and run away to Rome to hide. But while there, Onesimus met Paul and gave his heart to Jesus. Then he decided to return to his master to make things right again.

So Paul writes, "I thank God always, making mention of you in my prayers." Then he explained that Onesimus was no longer a slave, but a brother in Christ. He asked Philemon to welcome Onesimus home as he would welcome Paul himself. "If he has done you any wrong," Paul writes, "or if he owes you any money, charge it to me and I will pay it back." Paul loved Onesimus and prayed for his safe return.

Affirmation:
I will pray
for my friends!

COLLECT ALL 10

Word & Song AUDIO BOOK

Available in Your Favorite Christian Bookstore.

We hope you enjoyed this Word & Song Storybook.